P9-CCE-355

Hear Us…

Grayla H. Reneau

Hear Us...

✦

Word Prayers

Gary P. Melton Sr.

iUniverse, Inc.
New York Lincoln Shanghai

Hear Us...
Word Prayers

Copyright © 2005 by Gary P. Melton Sr.

All rights reserved. No part of this book may be used or reproduced by any means, graphic, electronic, or mechanical, including photocopying, recording, taping or by any information storage retrieval system without the written permission of the publisher except in the case of brief quotations embodied in critical articles and reviews.

iUniverse books may be ordered through booksellers or by contacting:

iUniverse
2021 Pine Lake Road, Suite 100
Lincoln, NE 68512
www.iuniverse.com
1-800-Authors (1-800-288-4677)

ISBN-13: 978-0-595-35803-8 (pbk)
ISBN-13: 978-0-595-80271-5 (ebk)
ISBN-10: 0-595-35803-9 (pbk)
ISBN-10: 0-595-80271-0 (ebk)

Printed in the United States of America

Contents

Preface . . . .*xi*

Prayer for Courage 1

Prayer Against Fear 2

Prayer not to Doubt 4

Prayer for Your Enemies 5

Forgiveness from God 6

Forgiveness of Each Other 7

Prayer Against Depression 8

How to be Born Again 9

Prayer When you are Lonely 11

Miracles 12

Safety in Christ 13

Faith 14

Protection 15

Victims of Crimes 16

Prayer for Blessed Assurance 17

Prayer for Your Home 19

Self-Control 20

Yield Not to Temptation 21

Worship 23

Comfort 25

Loss of Loved One 26

Prayer for the Church 27

Compassion 28

Healing 29

Anger 31

Confidence 32

Conformity 33

Demons 34

In Times of Discouragement 35

A Prayer for Faith 36

Receiving Gifts from God 37

Prayer for Giving 39

Prayer for Achieving Goals 40

Prayer for Freedom From Guilt 41

Prayer for Humility 42

Prayer of Love 43

Prayer for Your Marriage 44

Prayer for Obedience 46

Prayer for Patience 47

Prayer for Salvation 48

Prayer for Peace 49

Prayer Against Peer Pressure 50

Prayer of Thanks 51

Prayer for Godly Thoughts 52

Prayer for Trusting the Lord 53

Prayer for Wisdom 54

Prayer for God's Guidance 55

ACKNOWLEDGEMENT

To God, my wife Vicky, my children Jasmine, Gary Paul, Miles, and Malachi

Preface

"Put Me in remembrance: let us plead together." Isaiah 43:26. Word prayers, for lack of a better word, are powerful. God desires to have communication with his people and let's face it, sometimes we don't know what to say. Have you ever been going through so much that it seems you can't utter a word? Have you ever been so angry that you find it difficult to pray? Perhaps you are a new Christian who just doesn't know what to pray for. Perhaps you're an old Christian who knows the value of Word Prayers in spiritual warfare. Whatever position you find you find yourself in, there is one thing that is for sure; you need to PRAY. The most powerful prayers you can pray are those that remind God of his Word.

Each of the prayers written in this book are scriptures that have been put together to address various topics in your life. Don't be shocked that the scripture and verse are not noted. These prayers are meant to be prayed in the easiest manner possible, so they are written without any breaks. (A fun study you may want to complete is matching the scripture with the book, chapter, and verse.) You can replace the I's in the prayers with we, he with she, us with them, however they need to be utilized. No scriptures have been changed other than in tense (past, present, future) although some are written in the New International Version (NIV) of the King James Bible.

Praying the Word of God is so valuable because you are using the language that God is very used to hearing. You are essentially reminding God of his word and how it is meant to be effectual in your life. In your journey into living a total Christian life, you begin to sound like a Christian (ie. Christ like) as well as look like one in your daily goings.

These prayers are meant to start you off in your prayer life, strengthen your prayer life, or greatly enhance an established prayer life. It is written that the *"fervent, effectual prayers of the righteous avail much."* Attend church, bible studies, youth meetings, whatever it takes to achieve the righteousness of God and watch how Word Prayers can change your life.

Prayer for Courage

Glory be to God on High and on Earth peace and good will towards men. I praise you Lord, I bless you, and I give thanks to you for your great glory; for your magnificence, and for your mercy. Thank you for being God of all, all by yourself.

Lord help me to be strong and of good courage, to fear not, nor be afraid of them: for the Lord my God, he that is, goes with me; he will not fail me nor forsake me. Only allow me Lord to be strong and very courageous, that I may observe and do according to all law, which Moses your servant commanded me: turn not from it to the right hand nor to the left, that I may prosper wherever I go. Allow me Lord to be strong and fight bravely for my people and the cities of our God. I know the Lord will do what is good in his sight. Help me to be strong and courageous, to not be afraid or dismayed for any principality nor the multitude that is with them: for there will be more with me than with them: With them is the arm of flesh; but with me is the Lord my God to help me and to fight my battles.

I know that Christ is faithful as a son over God's house. And I am his house, if I hold on to my courage and the hope which I boast. This I ask in the matchless name of Jesus. Amen

Prayer Against Fear

Glory be to God on High and on Earth peace and good will towards men. I praise you Lord, I bless you, and I give thanks to you for your great glory; for your magnificence, and for your mercy. Thank you for being God of all, all by yourself.

Lord, I know you are my light and my salvation; whom shall I fear? You are the strength of my life of whom shall I be afraid? You have said Lord, to fear not: for you have redeemed me and called me by my name; I belong to you. When I pass through the waters you will be with me and the rivers will not drown me; when I walk through the fire I will not be burned; neither will the flame kindle on me. I looked for you Lord and you heard me, and delivered me from all my fears. You have left me your peace; you have given me your peace: the world cannot give me peace but you have given it to me. Let not my heart be troubled, neither let it be afraid. Help me Lord to fear not, for you are with me: to be not dismayed; for you are my God: I thank you Lord for you will strengthen me, help me, and uphold me with the right hand of your righteousness. For you have not given me a spirit of fear; but of power, and of love, and of sound mind. And although I may walk through the valley of the shadow of death, I will fear no evil, for you are with me. Lord, you have said, you will never leave me nor forsake me. You are my helper, and I will not be afraid of what man shall do to me.

Help me Lord not to be anxious about anything, but in every-thing, by prayer and petition, with thanksgiving I will present my request to God. And the peace of God that transcends all understanding, will guard my heart and mind in Christ Jesus. This I ask in the matchless name of Jesus. Amen.

Prayer not to Doubt

Glory be to God on High and on Earth peace and good will towards men. I praise you Lord, I bless you, and I give thanks to you for your great glory; for your magnificence, and for your mercy. Thank you for being God of all, all by yourself.

Lord, you have said that a double minded man is unstable in all his ways. Help me Lord to stop doubting and just believe. You told Thomas that he believed only when he saw: you said blessed are those who have not seen and yet believe. Help me to be that blessed person. Broaden my faith for without faith it is impossible to please you Lord. Help me to diligently seek you. Your Word Lord, is eternal; it stands firm in the heavens. Your faithfulness continues through all generations. Instruct me Lord and teach me the way in which to go: Guide me with your eye. I lack wisdom Lord and I ask that you give it to me liberally and unbraided: I know that if I ask, you will give. So I ask in faith, unwavering.

Wherefore seeing that I am compassed about with so great a cloud of witness, let me lay aside every weight, and the sin which so easily besets me, and let me run with patience the race that is set before me. Looking unto Jesus the author and finisher of my faith. This I ask in the matchless name of Jesus. Amen

Prayer for Your Enemies

Glory be to God on High and on Earth peace and good will towards men. I praise you Lord, I bless you, and I give thanks to you for your great glory; for your magnificence, and for your mercy. Thank you for being God of all, all by yourself.

Lord, bless them that curse me and I will pray for those that despitefully use me. To him that hits me on one cheek, I will offer the other also; and whoever takes my cloak I will not forbid them, but give my coat also. Lord, help me not to repay anyone evil for evil. I will be careful to do what is right in the eyes of everybody. If it is possible, as far as it depends on you, I will live at peace with everyone. I will not take revenge, but I will leave room for God's wrath, for it is written, "It is mine to avenge; I will repay," says the Lord. Help me Lord to love my enemies, bless them that curse me, do good to them that hate me, and persecuted me, and pray for them which despitefully use me. Lord, help me to forgive my brother not until seven times, but seventy times seven. Help me to forgive Lord as I have been forgiven. I will boldly say the Lord is my helper and I will not fear what man shall do unto me. Lord, when my enemies come to me one way, have them flee seven different ways. Through you Lord I will do valiantly: for you shall tread down my enemies.

I love you Lord, therefore I hate evil, for you guard the lives of your faithful ones and deliver us from the hands of the wicked. This I ask in the matchless name of Jesus. Amen

Forgiveness from God

Glory be to God on High and on Earth peace and good will towards men. I praise you Lord, I bless you, and I give thanks to you for your great glory; for your magnificence, and for your mercy. Thank you for being God of all, all by yourself.

Have mercy upon me, O God, according to thy lovingkindness: according unto the multitude of thy tender mercies, blot out my transgressions. Wash me thoroughly from my iniquity, and cleanse me from my sin. You said you would be merciful Lord, to my unrighteousness, and my sins and iniquities you will remember no more. I am wicked Lord, but I have forsaken my way and my thoughts and returned to you Lord. Have mercy upon me and I know you will abundantly pardon me. I confess and forsake my sins; cleanse me Lord, from all unrighteousness. Praise the Lord! Oh, my soul and I will not forget all of his benefits—who forgives all my sins and heals all of my diseases, who redeems my life from the pit and crowns me with love and compassion, who satisfies my desires with good things so that my youth is renewed like the eagle's.

Have Mercy upon me Lord, and please remember my sins no more. This I ask in the matchless name of Jesus. Amen.

Forgiveness of Each Other

Glory be to God on High and on Earth peace and good will towards men. I praise you Lord, I bless you, and I give thanks to you for your great glory; for your magnificence, and for your mercy. Thank you for being God of all, all by yourself.

Lord, you have said, "Blessed are the merciful, for they shall obtain mercy". As I stand praying, help me to forgive if I have anything against another: that my Father which is in heaven may forgive my trespasses. Help me to love my enemies, and do good, and lend, hoping for nothing to gain. If my enemy is hungry, I will give him to eat; if he is thirsty I will give him water to drink: by doing this I will heap fiery coals on his head and the Lord will reward me. If my brother trespasses against me, help me to rebuke him and if he repents I will forgive him.

Help me to be kind to others, tenderhearted, forgiving one another, even as God for Christ's sake forgave me. This I ask in the matchless name of Jesus. Amen.

Prayer Against Depression

Glory be to God on High and on Earth peace and good will towards men. I praise you Lord, I bless you, and I give thanks to you for your great glory; for your magnificence, and for your mercy. Thank you for being God of all, all by yourself.

Greater is he that is within me that he that is in the world. My soul Lord is cast down; it is disquieted within me. Restore my hope Lord God: for I will yet and still praise you. My spirit sustains me in sickness, but a crushed spirit Lord, I cannot bear. But I hear you saying Lord, that all power is given unto you in heaven and in earth. Keep me in perfect peace Lord, my mind is stayed on you. Whatsoever things are true, whatsoever things are honest, whatsoever things are just, whatsoever things are pure, whatsoever things are lovely, whatsoever things are of a good report; if there be any virtue, and if there be any praise, I will think on these things. Lord you give power to the faint, and to them that have no might, you increase their strength. Increase my strength today Lord. You have born all my grief's Lord, and carried away my sorrows: yet I did not esteem you stricken, smitten of God, and afflicted. But you were wounded for my transgressions, you were bruised for my iniquities: the chastisement of my peace was upon you; and with your stripes I am healed. For the joy of the Lord is my strength.

Peace you have left with me. Your Peace have you given me and I say thank you. This I pray in the matchless name of Jesus. Amen.

How to be Born Again

Glory be to God on High and on Earth peace and good will towards men. I praise you Lord, I bless you, and I give thanks to you for your great glory; for your magnificence, and for your mercy. Thank you for being God of all, all by yourself.

Lord, I am dead in trespasses and sins: in the past I have walked according to the course of this world, according to the prince of the power of the air, the spirit that works in the children of disobedience: I have fulfilled the desires of the flesh and of the mind; and was by nature one of the children of the wrath. But God you are rich in mercy, for with your great love you loved me. Even when I was dead in sins, you have quickened me together with Christ, for it is by grace I am saved. You have raised me up and made me to sit with Christ in heavenly places. For by grace I am saved through faith; not of myself: it is the gift of God: not of works lest I should boast. Jesus you bore my sins in your body on the tree, so that I might die to sins, and live for righteousness; by his wounds I have been healed. There is therefore now no condemnation to them which are in Christ Jesus, who walk not after the flesh, but after the Spirit. For that which is born of the flesh is flesh and that which is born of the Spirit is spirit. It is now that I confess with my mouth the Lord Jesus, and believe in my heart that God has raised him from the dead, and accept that I am saved.

For with the heart, man believes unto righteousness; and with the mouth confession is made unto salvation. This I pray in the name of Jesus. Amen.

Now that you have accepted the Lord Jesus Christ as your Savior, pray this prayer with me:

Lord, see that I have purified my soul in obeying the truth through the Spirit unto unfeigned love of the brethren, help us to love one another with a pure heart fervently: being born again, not of corruptible seed, but of incorruptible, by the word of God, which lives and abides forever. This I pray in the name of Jesus. Amen

Prayer When you are Lonely

Glory be to God on High and on Earth peace and good will towards men. I praise you Lord, I bless you, and I give thanks to you for your great glory; for your magnificence, and for your mercy. Thank you for being God of all, all by yourself.

I am complete in him, which is the head of all principality and power. God you are my refuge and strength a very present help in trouble. Therefore I will not fear, though the earth be removed and though the mountains be carried into the midst of the sea; though the waters thereof roar and be troubled, though the mountains shake with the swelling thereof. I know you are with me, and will keep me in all places that I go. You will not leave me comfortless, you will always come to me. I know you will never leave me nor forsake me, so I may boldly say that the Lord is my helper and I will not fear what man should do to me. And even though, I may walk through the valley of the shadow of death, I know that you are with me.

You have said, "Lo, I am with you always. Even unto the ends of the world. Here my prayer oh, Lord. This I pray in Jesus name. Amen.

Miracles

Glory be to God on High and on Earth peace and good will towards men. I praise you Lord, I bless you, and I give thanks to you for your great glory; for your magnificence, and for your mercy. Thank you for being God of all, all by yourself.

Lord, you are the God who performs miracles; you display your power among your people. I will seek you Lord and your strength: I will seek your face evermore. I will remember the marvelous works that you have done; your wonders, and the judgments of your mouth. I've read how in the same hour you cured many infirmities and plagues, and evil spirits; and to many the blind were given sight. You demonstrated that the works you do in your father's name, bear witness of you. This is a wicked generation. It asks for a miraculous sign, but none will be given except the sign of Jonah. For as Jonah was a sign to the Ninevites so also will the Son of Man be to this generation. For the Jews require a sign, and the Greeks seek after wisdom: But we preach Christ crucified. Lord, testify to your salvation by signs, wonders, various miracles, and gifts of the Holy Spirit distributed according to your will. Let your will be done in the mighty and matchless name of Jesus I pray. Amen.

Safety in Christ

Glory be to God on High and on Earth peace and good will towards men. I praise you Lord, I bless you, and I give thanks to you for your great glory; for your magnificence, and for your mercy. Thank you for being God of all, all by yourself.

Lord, I confess that you are Jesus the Christ, and you are the same yesterday, today, and evermore. I am made partaker of Christ, if I can hold the beginning of my confidence steadfast unto the end. Help me therefore, to give earnest heed to the things that I have heard, for it is impossible for those who were once enlightened, and have tasted the heavenly gift, and were made partakers of the Holy Ghost, and have tasted the good word of God, and the powers of the world to come, to fall away and be brought back to repentance. Help me Lord, to keep my hand to the plow, so that I may continue in faith, grounded and settled and not moved away from the hope of the gospel. Help me Lord to hold on to the profession of my faith, without wavering. You Lord, search all hearts and understand all the imaginations of thoughts: if I seek you, you will find me. Lord, I will give diligence to my calling and make my election sure, for I know if I do these things I will never fall. I know if I overcome, I will inherit all things; and you will be my God and I your son.

I will continue Lord in your goodness, I shall endure to the end, for I know that you are not willing that any should perish, but for all to come to repentance. In the knowledge of my Lord and Savior Jesus Christ I will continue to grow in grace. This I pray in Jesus name. Amen

Faith

Glory be to God on High and on Earth peace and good will towards men. I praise you Lord, I bless you, and I give thanks to you for your great glory; for your magnificence, and for your mercy. Thank you for being God of all, all by yourself.

Lord, I know without faith it is impossible to please you, and that I must believe in you for you are a rewarder of them that do diligently seek after you. I know that faith comes by hearing, and hearing by the word of God. Help me to not cast away my confidence, which has great recompense of reward, but allow me when I pray, to believe that I have received, and I know I shall have them. I will ask in faith Lord, nothing wavering so that the trail of my faith, being more precious than of gold that can perish, though it be tried with fire, might be found unto praise, honor, and glory at the appearing of Jesus Christ. I know that according to my faith, things shall be done, and it is my faith that will make me whole. Help me to fight the good fight of faith, and lay hold on eternal life. Whatsoever I ask Lord, I will receive of you, because I have kept your commandments, and do those things which are pleasing in your sight. Help me each day to take the shield of faith, so I will be able to quench all of the fiery darts of the wicked.

Lord, I want to fight the good fight, finish my course and keep the faith. This I will accomplish, God being my helper, in the mighty and matchless name of Jesus I pray. Amen.

Protection

Glory be to God on High and on Earth peace and good will towards men. I praise you Lord, I bless you, and I give thanks to you for your great glory; for your magnificence, and for your mercy. Thank you for being God of all, all by yourself.

Lord, allow the angel of the Lord to encamp round about me and deliver me. You have commanded me Lord to be strong and of good courage; to be not afraid, nor dismayed; for you Lord are with me wherever I go. You have given me Lord, power to tread on serpents and scorpions, and over all the power of the enemy: and nothing shall by any means hurt me. You, my eternal God, are my refuge and underneath are the everlasting arms. I will lift up my eyes to the hills, from where comes my help. My help comes from the Lord, which has made heaven and earth. Lord do not suffer my foot to be moved; don't slumber nor sleep. Watch over me, be the shade at my right hand; the sun will not harm me by day, nor the moon by night. Keep me from all harm—watch over my life; watch over my coming and going. In Jesus' name I pray. Amen.

Victims of Crimes

Glory be to God on High and on Earth peace and good will towards men. I praise you Lord, I bless you, and I give thanks to you for your great glory; for your magnificence, and for your mercy. Thank you for being God of all, all by yourself.

Lord, when my mother and my father have forsaken me, you said you would take me up. Lord, help me to have no fear; because you are with me: help me to not be dismayed; because you are my God: strengthen me Lord; help me Lord; hold me up with your right hand of righteousness. All those who are incensed against me, make them ashamed and confounded. Hold my right hand Lord and comfort me by saying "do not fear, I will help you". Help me not to be anxious about anything, but in everything, by prayer and petition: with thanksgiving, I will present my request to you.

Please allow the peace of God, which transcends all understanding, guard my heart and mind in Christ Jesus. This I pray in the mighty name of Jesus. Amen.

Prayer for Blessed Assurance

Glory be to God on High and on Earth peace and good will towards men. I praise you Lord, I bless you, and I give thanks to you for your great glory; for your magnificence, and for your mercy. Thank you for being God of all, all by yourself.

Lord, you have said that he that believeth on the Son has everlasting life, and he that does not believe has not life. Help me to believe on the name of the Son of God, that I may have eternal life. Help me to believe according to the eternal purpose in Christ Jesus my Lord: in whom I have boldness and access with confidence by faith of him. Help me to know, that I am from the truth, and to ensure my heart before him. For if my heart condemns me, God is greater than my heart and knows all things. Do not let my heart condemn me, so I may show confidence toward God. I know Heavenly Father that the redeemer lives and that he will stand at the latter day upon the earth: and after my skin worms destroy this body, yet in my flesh I will see God: who I will see for myself, my eyes will behold, and not another. I will draw near Lord, with a true heart in full assurance of faith, having my heart sprinkled from an evil conscience, and my body washed with pure water. Set me apart Lord, for your service: hear me Lord, when I call on you. Holy Spirit testify with my spirit that I am God's child. For I am persuaded, that neither death, nor life, nor angels, nor principalities, nor powers, nor things present, nor things to come, nor height, nor depth, nor any other creature, will be able to separate me from the love of God, which is in Christ Jesus my Lord.

I am not ashamed: for I know whom I have believed, and am persuaded that he is able to keep that which I have committed unto him against that day. This I pray in the name of Jesus. Amen.

Prayer for Your Home

Glory be to God on High and on Earth peace and good will towards men. I praise you Lord, I bless you, and I give thanks to you for your great glory; for your magnificence, and for your mercy. Thank you for being God of all, all by yourself.

Lord, you have given commandments to be upon my heart. Help me to impress them upon my children. Have me to talk about them when I am at home, when I walk down the road, when I lie down and when I get up. I know you Lord, and you will command me and my household after you, and we will keep the way Lord. Help me to train up my children in the way they should go: and when they are old, they will not depart from it. Lord, I will behave myself wisely in a perfect way. I will walk within my house with a perfect heart. I will carefully obey all these regulations you have given, so it will always go well with me and my children after me, because I am doing what is right in the eyes of the Lord my God.

Lord, bless my house, for better is a dry morsel, and quietness therewith, than a house full of sacrifices and strife. This I pray in the name of Jesus. Amen.

Self-Control

Glory be to God on High and on Earth peace and good will towards men. I praise you Lord, I bless you, and I give thanks to you for your great glory; for your magnificence, and for your mercy. Thank you for being God of all, all by yourself.

Lord, it is written, that a fool gives full vent to his anger, but a wise man keeps himself under control. For this reason, help me to make every effort to add to my faith goodness; and to goodness, knowledge; and to knowledge, self-control, and perseverance; and to perseverance, godliness; and to godliness, brotherly kindness; and to brotherly kindness, love. For if I can possess these qualities in increasing measure, they will keep me from being ineffective and unproductive in my knowledge of my Lord Jesus Christ. Help me to keep my body under subjection. Judge me O Lord; for I have walked in my integrity: I have trusted in the Lord; therefore I will not slide. Examine me, O Lord, and prove me; try my reins and my heart. Help me to be strong in the Lord, and in the power of his might. To put on the whole armor of God, that I may be able to stand against the wiles of the devil. For I wrestle not against flesh and blood, but against principalities, against powers, against the rulers of the darkness of this world, against spiritual wickedness in high places.

It is written, "Blessed is the man that endures temptation: for when he is tried, he shall receive the crown of life, which the Lord has promised to them that love him". Help me to be this blessed person, in the name of Jesus I pray. Amen.

Yield Not to Temptation

Glory be to God on High and on Earth peace and good will towards men. I praise you Lord, I bless you, and I give thanks to you for your great glory; for your magnificence, and for your mercy. Thank you for being God of all, all by yourself.

Lord, you know how to deliver the godly out of temptations, and to preserve the unjust unto the day of judgment. Knowing this, that the trying of my faith works patience. Help me to let patience have her perfect work, that I may be perfect and entire, wanting nothing. God, I know that you are faithful; you will never suffer me to be tempted above what I am able; but you will, with the temptation, make a way to escape, that I may be able to bear it. If sinners entice me, help me not to consent. Help me Lord, to watch and pray, so that I won't enter into temptation: for I know that the spirit is willing, but the flesh is weak. Lord, because I have kept the word of my patience, you will also keep me from the hour of temptation. For I do not have a high priest which cannot be touched with the feeling of my infirmities; but was in all points tempted like I am, yet without sin. Blessed is the man that endures temptation: for when he is tried, he shall receive the crown of life, which the Lord has promised to them that love him. Lord, I will not say when I am tempted, that I am tempted by God: for I know that God cannot be tempted with evil, neither does he tempt any man.

These things have you spoken to me Lord, that in you I might have peace. In the world I know I shall have tribulation: but I will be of good cheer for you have overcome the world. Lord, I pray that I do not enter into temptation, in the mighty name of Jesus. Amen.

Worship

Glory be to God on High and on Earth peace and good will towards men. I praise you Lord, I bless you, and I give thanks to you for your great glory; for your magnificence, and for your mercy. Thank you for being God of all, all by yourself.

Lord, you have said to worship no other god: for the Lord whose name is Jealous, is a jealous God. I desire to give to you Lord the glory due unto your name; I will worship you in the beauty of holiness. I will enter your gates with thanksgiving, and into your courts with praise: I will be thankful to you Lord, and bless your name. For the hour will come and now is when true worshippers shall worship the Father in spirit and in truth: for this is what you seek, worship to you. God I know you are a spirit and I must worship you in spirit and in truth. So, Lord, I sing to you a new song, for you are great, and greatly to be praised: you are feared above all gods. Honor and majesty are before you: strength and beauty are in your sanctuary. I will give to you Lord the glory due to your name: I will bring an offering and come into your courts. O worship the Lord in the beauty of holiness: fear before him, all the earth. Let the heavens rejoice, and let the earth be glad; let the sea roar, and the fullness thereof. The four and twenty elders fell down before him that sat upon the throne, and worshipped him that lives for ever and ever, and cast their crowns before the throne, saying, "Thou art worthy, O Lord, to receive glory and honor and power: for you have created all things, and for thy pleasure they were created. Then I looked and heard the voice of many angels, numbering thousands upon thousands, and ten thousand times ten thousand. They encircled the throne, the living creatures and the elders. With a loud voice they sang, "Worthy is the Lamb, who was slain, to receive power and wealth and wisdom and strength and honor and glory and praise!" Then I heard every creature in heaven and on earth and on the sea, and all that is in them, singing: "To him who sits on the throne and to the Lamb be praise and honor and glory and power, for ever and ever!"

Holy, holy, holy, Lord God Almighty, which was, and is, and is to come. In Jesus name this is my prayer. Amen.

Comfort

Glory be to God on High and on Earth peace and good will towards men. I praise you Lord, I bless you, and I give thanks to you for your great glory; for your magnificence, and for your mercy. Thank you for being God of all, all by yourself.

Lord, you have promised never to leave me nor forsake me. I come to you Lord, for I have labored and am heavy laden. Lord, please give me rest. Remember the word you have given to me which gives me hope. This is my comfort in my affliction: for your Word has quickened me. When my father and my mother have forsaken me, you said you would take me up. You have prayed to the Father, Jesus, and he has sent another Comforter, that will abide with me forever and I say thank you. Blessed be God, even the Father of my Lord Jesus Christ, the Father of mercies, and the God of all comfort; who comforts me in all tribulation, that I may be able to comfort them which are in any trouble, by the comfort wherewith I myself am comforted of God.

Lord, allow me to take your yoke upon me, and learn of you, so that I may find rest unto my soul. For your yoke is easy and your burden is light. This I ask in the mighty name of Jesus. Amen.

Loss of Loved One

Glory be to God on High and on Earth peace and good will towards men. I praise you Lord, I bless you, and I give thanks to you for your great glory; for your magnificence, and for your mercy. Thank you for being God of all, all by yourself.

Lord, you said that you would not have us to be ignorant concerning those which are asleep. That we do not sorrow as those which have no hope. Knowing that while we are at home in the body, we are absent from the Lord: We are confident that to be absent from the body, is to be present with the Lord. Yea, though I walk through the valley of the shadow of death I will fear no evil for you are with me. Precious in the sight of the Lord is the death of his saints. Jesus, you are the resurrection, and the life: he that believes in you though they were dead, yet shall they live: And whosoever lives and believes in you shall never die. Help us to believe this. For if we believe that Jesus died and rose again, even those that sleep in Jesus, God will bring with him. Now we are the sons of God, and it does not yet appear what we shall be: but we know that, when he shall appear, we shall be like him; for we shall see him as he is. And God shall wipe away all the tears from their eyes; and there shall be no more death, neither sorrow, nor crying, neither shall there be any more pain: for the former things are passed away.

O death, where is your sting? O, grave where is your victory? The sting of death is sin; and the strength of sin is the law. But thanks be to God, which gives us the victory through our Lord Jesus Christ. This I pray in the matchless name of Jesus. Amen.

Prayer for the Church

Glory be to God on High and on Earth peace and good will towards men. I praise you Lord, I bless you, and I give thanks to you for your great glory; for your magnificence, and for your mercy. Thank you for being God of all, all by yourself.

Jesus, you are the head of the church: and you are the savior of the body. You loved the church, and gave yourself for it. For as the body is one, it has many members, and all the members of the body, being many, are one body: so also is Christ. For by one Spirit we are all baptized into one body and been made to drink into one Spirit. For the body is not one member, but many. We also as lively stones, have built up a spiritual house, a holy priesthood, to offer up spiritual sacrifices, acceptable to God by Jesus Christ. We are a chosen generation, a royal priesthood, a holy nation, a peculiar people, that we should show forth the praises of him who called us out of darkness into his marvelous light. Let us not give up meeting together, as some are in the habit of doing, but let us encourage one another—and all the more as we see the Day approaching. Let us continue steadfastly in the apostles' doctrine and fellowship, and in breaking bread, and in prayers. The Lord knows who are his. Let everyone that names the name of Christ depart from iniquity.

Lord, upon this rock build your Church; and we know that the gates of hell will not prevail against it. This I pray in the mighty and matchless name of Jesus. Amen.

Compassion

Glory be to God on High and on Earth peace and good will towards men. I praise you Lord, I bless you, and I give thanks to you for your great glory; for your magnificence, and for your mercy. Thank you for being God of all, all by yourself.

Lord, help me to administer true justice; to show mercy and compassion to others: to not alienate the widow, or the fatherless, or the poor. To not think evil of another. As God's chosen people, holy and dearly loved, help me to clothe myself with compassion, kindness, humility, gentleness, and patience. Help me Lord to be a good man that shows favor and lends: to guide my affairs with discretion, that my righteous may endure forever.

This I pray in the mighty and matchless name of Jesus. Amen.

Healing

Glory be to God on High and on Earth peace and good will towards men. I praise you Lord, I bless you, and I give thanks to you for your great glory; for your magnificence, and for your mercy. Thank you for being God of all, all by yourself.

Lord, I know I am fearfully and wonderfully made and that my body is the temple of the Holy Ghost. Many are the afflictions of the righteous, but Lord, you deliver me from them all. Bless O Lord, O my soul, and forget not all your benefits, who forgives all iniquities and heals all my diseases. You were wounded for my transgressions, you were bruised for my iniquities: the chastisement of my people was upon you; and with your stripes, I am healed. Help me to diligently hearken to your voice, Lord, and do what is right in your sight, give ear to your commandments, and keep all of your statutes, and you promised to put none of the diseases on me that you have brought upon the Egyptians: for you are he Lord that heals me. Lord, it is written that if there are any sick among us, to call for the elders of the church; to pray over them, anointing them with oil in the name of the Lord; and the prayer of faith shall save the sick, and the Lord shall raise them up. Whatsoever I ask, I shall receive of you Lord, because I have kept your commandments, and do those things that are pleasing in your sight. Please make me whole Lord.

Lord, I know that you wish above all things that I may prosper and be in health, even as my soul prospers. You are the strength of my life. I pray this prayer believing that I will receive, and I know Lord, you will give them. In the mighty name of Jesus I pray. Amen.

Anger

Glory be to God on High and on Earth peace and good will towards men. I praise you Lord, I bless you, and I give thanks to you for your great glory; for your magnificence, and for your mercy. Thank you for being God of all, all by yourself.

Lord, it is written that I should cease from anger and forsake wrath: to not worry myself in any way to do evil. A fool gives full vent to his anger but a wise man keeps himself under control. Help me to give a soft answer to turn away wrath. Let all bitterness, wrath, anger, clamor, and evil speaking, be put away from me with all malice. I will make no friendship with an angry man; with an angry man I will not go, so to not learn his ways, and ensnare my soul. Help me when I am angry to not sin: I will not let the sun go down and still be angry: Neither will I give place to the devil.

Help me to keep my anger. In Jesus name I pray. Amen.

Confidence

Glory be to God on High and on Earth peace and good will towards men. I praise you Lord, I bless you, and I give thanks to you for your great glory; for your magnificence, and for your mercy. Thank you for being God of all, all by yourself.

Lord, be my confidence, for it is better to trust in the Lord than to put confidence in man. You have been my hope, my confidence since my youth. For I am the circumcision, which worship God in the spirit, and rejoice in Christ Jesus, and have no confidence in the flesh. I will not put my confidence in a friend or in a guide. For a son dishonors his father, the daughter will rise up against her mother, the daughter in law against her mother in law; a man's enemies are the men of his own house. Therefore, I will look to the Lord; I will wait for the God of my salvation; my God will hear me. For I am made a partaker of Christ, if I can hold the beginning of my confidence steadfast until the end. This is the confidence that I have in you, that, if I ask anything according to your will, you hear me: and if I know that you hear me, whatsoever I ask, I know that I have the petitions that I have desired of him.

And now I will abide in him; that when he shall appear, I may have confidence, and not be ashamed before him at his coming. This I pray in the mighty name of Jesus. Amen.

Conformity

Glory be to God on High and on Earth peace and good will towards men. I praise you Lord, I bless you, and I give thanks to you for your great glory; for your magnificence, and for your mercy. Thank you for being God of all, all by yourself.

By the mercies of my God, help me to present my body a living sacrifice, holy, acceptable unto God, which is my reasonable service. Help me Lord to be not conformed to this world, but to be transformed by the renewing of my mind, that I may prove what is that good, and acceptable, and perfect will of God. Help me not to conform with evil desires that I had when I was ignorant, but just as he who calls me is holy, help me to be holy in all that I do.

I will not be unequally yoked together with unbelievers: for righteousness has no relationship with unrighteousness, and light has no communion with darkness. Therefore, I will come out from them, and be separate. I will not touch the unclean thing; receive me Lord and be my Father. In the mighty and matchless name of Jesus I pray. Amen.

Demons

Glory be to God on High and on Earth peace and good will towards men. I praise you Lord, I bless you, and I give thanks to you for your great glory; for your magnificence, and for your mercy. Thank you for being God of all, all by yourself.

Lord, I know that we do not wrestle against flesh and blood, but against principalities, against powers, against the rulers of the darkness of this world, and against spiritual wickedness in high places. Wherefore, I put on the whole armor of God, that I may be able to withstand in the evil day, and having done all, to stand. I submit myself to God and resist the devil. I believe that there is one God; devils also believe and tremble. I thank you Lord for you have given me power and authority over all devils, and to cure diseases. Help me to be self-controlled and alert. For I know the enemy prowls around like a roaring lion looking for someone to devour. I will resist him standing firm in the faith. Every spirit that does not confess that Jesus Christ is come in the flesh is not of God.

I resist the devil and I know he will flee; I draw near to God in the name of Jesus I pray. Amen.

In Times of Discouragement

Glory be to God on High and on Earth peace and good will towards men. I praise you Lord, I bless you, and I give thanks to you for your great glory; for your magnificence, and for your mercy. Thank you for being God of all, all by yourself.

I cried unto God with my voice, even unto God with my voice; and he gave ear unto me. He healed my broken heart and bound up my wounds. The Lord God has set the land before me: and has told me to go up and possess it. He has said not to fear, neither to be discouraged, for they that wait on the Lord will renew their strength; they will mount up with wings as eagles; they will run, and not be weary; and they will walk and not faint. You have commanded me Lord to be strong and of good courage; to be not afraid, neither to be dismayed: for you are with me no matter where I go. I am troubled on every side but not distressed; I am perplexed, but not in despair. Knowing that he which raised up the Lord Jesus will raise up me also by Jesus, and will present me with you.

Hear me O Lord. For I know a broken and contrite heart, O God, you will not despise. This I pray in the mighty and matchless name of Jesus. Amen.

A Prayer for Faith

Glory be to God on High and on Earth peace and good will towards men. I praise you Lord, I bless you, and I give thanks to you for your great glory; for your magnificence, and for your mercy. Thank you for being God of all, all by yourself.

Lord, I know without faith is impossible to please God: for he that comes to God must believe that he is, and he is a rewarder of them that diligently seek him. Therefore, I am crucified with Christ: nevertheless I live; yet not I, but Christ lives in me: and the life in which I now live in the flesh, I live by the faith of the Son of God, who loved me, and gave himself for me. In this I rejoice even if now for a little while I have had to suffer various trials, so that the genuineness of my faith—being more precious than gold, that though perishable, is tested by fire—may be found to result in praise and glory and honor when Jesus Christ is revealed. Although I have not seen him, I love him; and rejoice with an indescribable and glorious joy, for I am receiving the outcome of my faith; the salvation of my soul. For by grace I am saved through faith; and not by myself: it is the gift of God: not of works, lest I should boast.

Therefore being justified by faith, I have peace with God through my Lord Jesus Christ. This I pray in Jesus name. Amen.

Receiving Gifts from God

Glory be to God on High and on Earth peace and good will towards men. I praise you Lord, I bless you, and I give thanks to you for your great glory; for your magnificence, and for your mercy. Thank you for being God of all, all by yourself.

Lord, you told the woman at the well, "If you knew the gift of God and who said it to you, you would give me to drink; and he would have given you living water". The gift of God is eternal life through Jesus Christ my Lord. If I then being evil, know how to give good gifts to my children: how much more will my heavenly Father give the Holy Spirit to them that ask them? Lord I ask for the gift of the Holy Spirit. I wait for the promise of the Father. I have repented and been baptized in the name of Jesus Christ for the remission of my sins, that I may receive the gift of the Holy Ghost. For you have promised this to me Lord, and to my children, and to all those that are far away. As many as you Lord God will call. Lord, reveal my gifts to me for each man has his own gift from God. We have different gifts, according to the grace given to us. But the manifestation of the Spirit is given to every man to profit for all. I am eager to have spiritual gifts, please let me excel in gifts that build up the church. Stir up the gift of God, which is in me, Lord. Allow me to use whatever gift I have received to serve others, faithfully administering God's grace in different forms. I will be sure not to neglect the gift that is within me, which was given by prophecy, with the laying on of the hands presbytery.

Every good gift and every perfect gift is from above, and comes down from the Father of Lights, with whom is no variableness, nor shadow of turning. God, you work in all gifts; allow me to receive your gifts in the mighty and matchless name of Jesus I pray. Amen.

Prayer for Giving

Glory be to God on High and on Earth peace and good will towards men. I praise you Lord, I bless you, and I give thanks to you for your great glory; for your magnificence, and for your mercy. Thank you for being God of all, all by yourself.

Lord, help me to remember the words you spoke when you said it is more blessed to give than to receive. Help me to give; not grudgingly, nor of necessity: for God you love a cheerful giver. Help me to be a righteous giver and not to spare, for freely have I received and freely I desire to give. I will honor you Lord with my wealth, with the first fruits of all my crops; then I know my barns will be filled to overflowing. I do not desire to rob you O God. Allow me to give my tithes and offering so that there will be meat in your house. I know you will open the windows of heaven and pour out a blessing, that there will not be enough room to receive it and you will rebuke the devourer for my sake.

I will give and I know I will receive; good measure, pressed down, shaken together, and running over, will men give unto my bosom. For with the measure I use, it will be measured to me. This I pray in the mighty name of Jesus. Amen.

Prayer for Achieving Goals

Glory be to God on High and on Earth peace and good will towards men. I praise you Lord, I bless you, and I give thanks to you for your great glory; for your magnificence, and for your mercy. Thank you for being God of all, all by yourself.

Lord, make it my goal to please you, whether I'm at home in the body or away from it. The goal of this command is love, which comes from a pure heart, a good conscience and a sincere faith. Let me not become weary in doing good, for at the proper time I will reap a harvest if I do not give up. Wherefore seeing I am also compassed about with so great a cloud of witness, I will lay aside every weight, and sin that so easily besets me, and I will run with patience the race that is set before me, looking to Jesus the author and finisher of my faith. I will commit my way to you, O Lord; trust in you; and you will bring it to pass. Not that I have already obtained all this, or have already been made perfect, but I press on to take hold of that for which Christ Jesus took hold of me. I do not consider myself yet to have taken hold of it. But one thing I do:

Forgetting what is behind and straining towards what is ahead, I press on toward the goal to win the prize for which God has called me heavenward in Christ Jesus. This I pray in Jesus' name. Amen.

Prayer for Freedom From Guilt

Glory be to God on High and on Earth peace and good will towards men. I praise you Lord, I bless you, and I give thanks to you for your great glory; for your magnificence, and for your mercy. Thank you for being God of all, all by yourself.

Lord, it is written that he that covers his sin will not prosper: but whoever confesses and forsakes his sin will have mercy. When I kept silent, my bones wasted through my groaning all day long. Then I acknowledged my sin to you and did not cover up my iniquity. I confessed my transgressions to you Lord and you forgave the guilt of my sin. Though my sins were as scarlet, you made them white as snow. As far as the east is from the west, is how far you moved my transgressions from me. My guilt has overwhelmed me like a burden to heavy to bear. But you Lord are gracious and merciful, and will not turn your face from me if I return to you. There is therefore now no condemnation to them which are in Christ Jesus, who does not walk after the flesh, but after the Spirit.

Therefore, since I have confidence to enter the Most Holy Place by the blood of Jesus, I will draw near to God with a sincere heart in full assurance of faith, having my heart sprinkled to cleanse me from a guilty conscience and having my body washed with pure water. This I pray in the mighty name of Jesus. Amen.

Prayer for Humility

Glory be to God on High and on Earth peace and good will towards men. I praise you Lord, I bless you, and I give thanks to you for your great glory; for your magnificence, and for your mercy. Thank you for being God of all, all by yourself.

Lord, let this mind be in me that is also in Christ Jesus: who being in the form of God, thought it not robbery to be equal with God: But made himself of no reputation, and took upon him the form of a servant, and was made in the likeness of men: and being found in fashion as a man, he humbled himself, and became obedient unto death, even the death of the cross. Help me to humble myself as a little child, humble myself under God's mighty hand, that he may lift me up in due time. For by humility and fear of the Lord are riches, and honor, and life. The fear of the Lord teaches a man wisdom, and humility comes before honor.

It is written "If my people, which are called by my name, will humble themselves and pray, and seek my face, and turn from their wicked ways; then will I hear from heaven, and will forgive their sin, and will heal their land. This I pray in the mighty and matchless name of Jesus. Amen.

Prayer of Love

Glory be to God on High and on Earth peace and good will towards men. I praise you Lord, I bless you, and I give thanks to you for your great glory; for your magnificence, and for your mercy. Thank you for being God of all, all by yourself.

A new commandment have you given me Lord. It is that I love everyone, as I love you. By this all men will know that I am a disciple of God. I will love everyone: for love is of God, and everyone that loves is born of God and knows God. I will not say I love God but hate my brother for I will be considered a liar. For how can I say I don't love my brother who I see everyday and love God whom I have not seen. Love must be sincere; hate what is evil; cling to what is good.

Love is patient, love is kind. It does not envy, it does not boast, it is not proud. It is not rude, it is not self-seeking, it is not easily angered, it keeps no record of wrongs. Love does not delight in evil but rejoices with the truth. It always protects, always trusts, always hopes, always preserves. Love never fails. This is my prayer, in the name of Jesus. Amen.

Prayer for Your Marriage

Glory be to God on High and on Earth peace and good will towards men. I praise you Lord, I bless you, and I give thanks to you for your great glory; for your magnificence, and for your mercy. Thank you for being God of all, all by yourself.

Lord, it is not good that the man should be alone; so you made a help meet for him. Therefore, shall a man leave his father and his mother and cleave to his wife; and they will be one flesh. Christ has redeemed us from the curse of the law, being made a curse for us. For we all are the children of God by faith in Christ Jesus. For as many of us have been baptized into Christ have put on Christ. There is neither bond or free, there is neither male or female: for we all are one in Christ Jesus. The man was not created for the woman but the woman for the man (the woman is the glory of the man). Nevertheless neither is the man without the woman or the woman without the man, in the Lord. For as the woman is of the man, the man is also of the woman: but all things are of God. Lord, you have said to us, that if two should agree on earth as touching anything we should ask, it will be done. If one should chase a thousand then two will put ten thousand to flight. Help us to submit to one another out of reverence for Christ. Wives to submit to your husbands. Husbands love your wives, even as Christ loved the church, and gave himself for it. Marriage is honorable in all, and the bed is undefiled, but whoremongers and adulterers God will judge.

Lord, help us to perform our marital duties to each other. The wife's body does not belong to her alone but also to her husband. In the same way the husband's body does not belong to him alone but also to his wife. Help us not to deprive one another except by mutual consent and for a time, so that we may devote ourselves to prayer. Then come together again so that Satan cannot tempt us because of our lack of self-control.

Lord, bless our marriage for we know unless the Lord builds a house, we labor in vain to build it ourselves. This we pray in the mighty name of Jesus. Amen.

Prayer for Obedience

Glory be to God on High and on Earth peace and good will towards men. I praise you Lord, I bless you, and I give thanks to you for your great glory; for your magnificence, and for your mercy. Thank you for being God of all, all by yourself.

Lord, it is written that it is far better to obey than to sacrifice, for rebellion is as the sin of witchcraft and stubbornness is as iniquity and idolatry. Help me to obey for he that says I know him and does not obey your commandments is a liar and the truth is not in him. Lord help me to bring into captivity every thought to the obedience of Christ. For the weapons of my warfare are not carnal, but mighty through God to the pulling down of strongholds; Casting down imaginations, and every high thing that exalts itself against the knowledge of God, and bringing into captivity every thought to the obedience of Christ. I will obey the voice of the Lord my God and do his commandments and his statutes that he has commanded of me on this day. If I love the Lord, I will keep his commandments. If I love the Lord, I will keep his words: and my Father will love me, and I will come to him, and make my abode with him. I will be a doer of the word and not just a hearer.

Not everyone that says Lord, Lord, will enter the kingdom of heaven; but he that does the will of my Father which is in heaven. Help me to continue to do your will Lord. In the mighty and matchless name of Jesus I pray. Amen.

Prayer for Patience

Glory be to God on High and on Earth peace and good will towards men. I praise you Lord, I bless you, and I give thanks to you for your great glory; for your magnificence, and for your mercy. Thank you for being God of all, all by yourself.

Lord, it is written that patience is one of the fruits of the Spirit and that the patient in spirit is better than the proud in spirit. Lord, grant me patience. Have me to glory in tribulations: always, knowing that tribulation works patience; and patience, experience, and experience, hope. Help me to be patient towards all men, never to render evil with evil to anyone, but follow that which is good. Love is patient, love is kind…it is not easily angered. I will be patient until the Lord's coming. I will not be weary in well doing: for in due season I will reap, if I don't faint.

Lord, I will rest in you, and wait patiently for you: I will not fret myself because of him that prospers in his own way, for I have need of patience, that after I have done God's will, I might receive the promise. This I pray in the name of Jesus. Amen.

Prayer for Salvation

Glory be to God on High and on Earth peace and good will towards men. I praise you Lord, I bless you, and I give thanks to you for your great glory; for your magnificence, and for your mercy. Thank you for being God of all, all by yourself.

Lord, it is written "For what will it profit a man, if he should gain the whole world, and lose his own soul. Christ Jesus came to the world to save sinners. Jesus said "I am not come to call the righteous, but sinners to repentance. All have sinned and come short of the glory of God. We are all as an unclean thing, all our righteousness as filthy rags. Therefore, whosoever will call on the name of the Lord will be saved. Lord, you said if I come you will in no wise cast me out. I accept Lord, that there is one God, and one mediator between God and man, the man Christ Jesus; who gave himself a ransom for me. So, I come boldly to the throne of grace, that I may obtain mercy, and find grace in the time of need. I am thirsty Lord, bid me to come to you and drink. The Lord is my strength and my song, and he has become my salvation: he is my God and I will exalt him.

Since I am now in Christ, I am a new creature: old things are passed away; behold, all things are become new. I heard you knocking at my door Lord. I hear your voice and open the door. Come in and let us eat together. Help me to overcome that I may have the right to sit with you on your throne, just as you overcame and sat down with God the Father on his throne. This I pray in the mighty and matchless name of Jesus. Amen.

Prayer for Peace

Glory be to God on High and on Earth peace and good will towards men. I praise you Lord, I bless you, and I give thanks to you for your great glory; for your magnificence, and for your mercy. Thank you for being God of all, all by yourself.

Lord, keep me in perfect peace, my mind stayed on you. I being justified by faith, I have peace with God through my Lord Jesus Christ and the peace of God, which passes all understanding shall keep my heart and mind through Jesus Christ. I will seek peace and pursue it Lord, for I know, blessed are the peacemakers for they will be called the children of God. God you have told me these things, so that in you I may have peace. In this world I will have trouble. But I take heart! For I know you have overcome the world.

I know that all things work together for good to them that love God, and are called according to his purpose. This I pray in the name of Jesus. Amen.

Prayer Against Peer Pressure

Glory be to God on High and on Earth peace and good will towards men. I praise you Lord, I bless you, and I give thanks to you for your great glory; for your magnificence, and for your mercy. Thank you for being God of all, all by yourself.

Lord, help me to walk worthy of God, who has called me unto his kingdom. Help me to be holy, for you are holy. For you have not called me to uncleanliness, but to holiness. Therefore, I will come out from them and be separate. I will touch no unclean thing and I will be received of God. I will not fashion myself to the former lusts in my ignorance. I will walk worthy of God, who has called me unto his kingdom and glory. In my heart I will set apart Christ as Lord, always prepared to give an answer to everyone who asks me to give a reason for the hope that I have. I will do this with gentleness and respect, keeping a clear conscience, so that those who speak maliciously against my good behavior in Christ may be ashamed of their slander.

God, in view of your mercy, I offer my body as a living sacrifice, holy and pleasing to you—this is my spiritual act of worship. I will not conform any longer to the pattern of this world, but I will be transformed by the renewing of my mind. Then I will be able to test and approve what God's will is—his good pleasing and perfect will. This I pray in the name of Jesus. Amen.

Prayer of Thanks

Glory be to God on High and on Earth peace and good will towards men. I praise you Lord, I bless you, and I give thanks to you for your great glory; for your magnificence, and for your mercy. Thank you for being God of all, all by yourself.

Lord, in everything I give thanks: for this is the will of God in Christ Jesus concerning me. I give thanks unto the Lord; call upon his name: and make known his deeds to the people. I will come before his presence with thanksgiving, and make a joyful noise unto him with psalms. I give thanks to the Lord; for he is good and his mercy endures forever.

Enter into his gates with thanksgiving, and into his courts with praise: be thankful to him and bless his name. I say, Amen: Blessing, and glory, and wisdom, and thanksgiving, and honor, power, and might, be to our God for ever and ever. Amen.

Prayer for Godly Thoughts

Glory be to God on High and on Earth peace and good will towards men. I praise you Lord, I bless you, and I give thanks to you for your great glory; for your magnificence, and for your mercy. Thank you for being God of all, all by yourself.

Lord, Search me O, God, and know my heart; try me and know my thoughts: and see if there is any wicked way in me, and lead me in the way forever. I know that no thought can be withheld from you. Create in me a clean heart, and renew a right spirit in me. Let the words of my mouth, and the meditations of my heart, be acceptable in your sight, O Lord, my strength and my redeemer. Set my affections on things above, not on things on the earth.

I will not be conformed to this world, but I will be transformed, by the renewing of my mind. Therefore, whatsoever things are true, whatsoever things are honest, whatsoever things are just, whatsoever things are pure, whatsoever things are lovely, whatsoever things are of good report; if there be any virtue, and if there be any praise, I will think on these things. In Jesus name it is my prayer. Amen.

Prayer for Trusting the Lord

Glory be to God on High and on Earth peace and good will towards men. I praise you Lord, I bless you, and I give thanks to you for your great glory; for your magnificence, and for your mercy. Thank you for being God of all, all by yourself.

O Lord my God, in you I put my trust: save me from all them that persecute me, and deliver me. Though he slay me, yet will I trust in him: but I will maintain mine own ways before him. I will trust in the Lord with all my heart; and lean not into my own understanding. In all my ways I will acknowledge him and he will direct my paths. I will trust in the God of my rock. He is my shield and the horn of my salvation, my high tower, and my refuge, my savior; you save me from violence. I will trust in the Lord, and do good; so I can dwell in the land, and be fed. I will delight myself also in the Lord and he will give me the desires of my heart. I will commit my ways to the Lord; trust also in him; and he will bring it to pass.

Some trust in chariots, and some in horses: but I will remember the name of the Lord my God. This I pray in the name of Jesus. Amen.

Prayer for Wisdom

Glory be to God on High and on Earth peace and good will towards men. I praise you Lord, I bless you, and I give thanks to you for your great glory; for your magnificence, and for your mercy. Thank you for being God of all, all by yourself.

Lord, it is written that if anyone lacks wisdom, let him ask of God, who gives to all men liberally, and does no chastise; and it will be given. Lord, let the word of Christ dwell in me richly in all wisdom; teaching and admonishing each other in psalms and hymns and spiritual songs, singing with grace in our hearts to the Lord. For the Lord gives wisdom: out of his mouth comes knowledge and understanding.

Help me Lord to be that blessed man that does not walk in the counsel of the ungodly, or stands in the way of sinners, or sits in the seat of the scornful. But let my delight be in the law of the Lord; and in his law will I meditate day and night. This I pray in the name of Jesus. Amen.

Prayer for God's Guidance

Glory be to God on High and on Earth peace and good will towards men. I praise you Lord, I bless you, and I give thanks to you for your great glory; for your magnificence, and for your mercy. Thank you for being God of all, all by yourself.

Lord, it is written that you will instruct me and teach me in the way I should go: you will guide me with your eye. Teach me your way, O Lord, and lead me in the plain path. I am meek Lord, guide me in judgment; for the meek you will teach in your way. I will trust in the Lord with all my heart: and will not lean to my own understanding. In all my ways I will acknowledge the Lord God, and he will direct my paths. Show me thy ways, O Lord; for you are the God of my salvation, on you I will wait. For the steps of a good man are ordered by the Lord. He leads in the paths of righteousness for his name's sake. For God is my God for ever and ever; he will be my guide even unto death. I will walk by faith and not by sight, for you are my rock and my fortress; therefore for your name's sake lead me and guide me. For as many that are led by the Spirit of God, are the sons of God.

Lord, I will commit to you whatever I do, and my plans will succeed. Your word, Lord, is a lamp unto my feet, and a light unto my path. Your kingdom come, Lord. Your will be done in earth as it is in heaven. This I pray in the mighty and matchless name of Jesus. Amen.

978-0-595-35803-8
0-595-35803-9

Printed in the United States
49639LVS00001B/1-15